LAST MINUTE REVISION

GCSE HIGHER MATHS
Booster

First published 2000
exclusively for WHSmith by

Hodder & Stoughton Educational
228 Euston Road
London NW1 3BH

A CIP record for this book is available from the British Library.

Text: Jane James
Illustrations: Helen Humphreys
Developed and edited by Hart McLeod

ISBN 0340 78126 2

Printed and bound by Hobbs The Printer, Totton, Hants

Angle properties of a circle

The angle in the centre is double the angle at the circumference
a = 2b

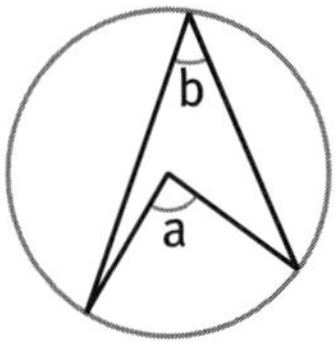

Angles at the circumference are the same
c = d

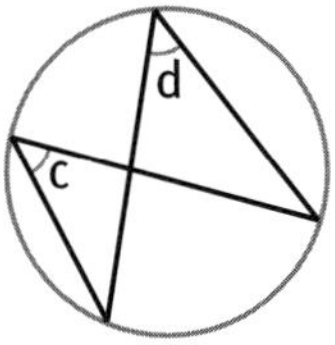

The angle in a semi-circle is a right angle

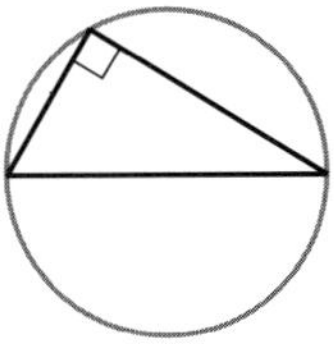

Opposite angles in a cyclic quadrilateral add up to 180°
a + c = 180°
b + d = 180°

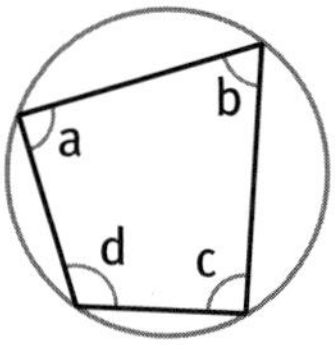

The tangent and the radius meet at 90°.

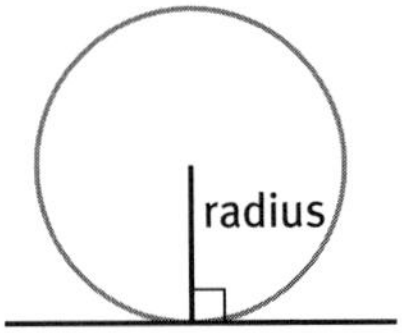

You can also look out for this isosceles triangle – two radii mean two sides the same length!

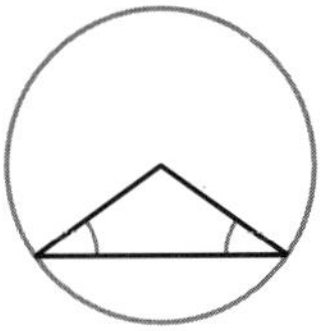

Angles and parallel lines

Alternate angles are equal
(Z angles) e = f

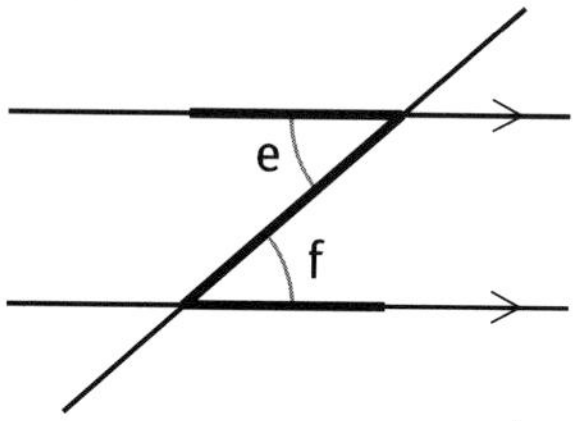

Corresponding angles are also equal
(F angles) g = h

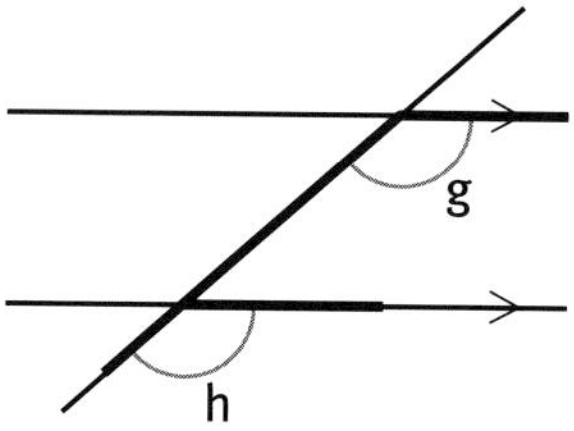

Interior angles add up to 180°
(C angles) j + k = 180°

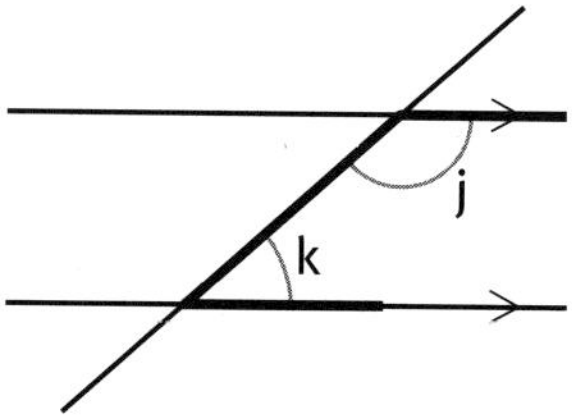

Arc length

The length of the arc is found by using the angle at the centre

Arc length = $\frac{a}{360} \times 2\pi r$

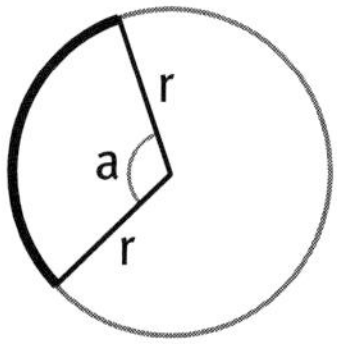

In this case the arc length is:

$\frac{60}{360} \times 2 \times \pi \times 2 = \frac{2\pi}{3}$ cm
$= 2.09$ cm

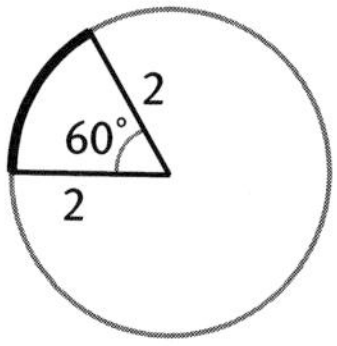

Make sure you can use these formulae correctly!

Triangle

Area = $\frac{1}{2}$ × base × vertical height
A = $\frac{1}{2} \times b \times h$

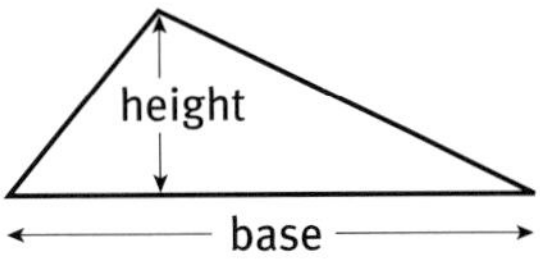

Parallelogram

Area = base × vertical height
A = $b \times h$

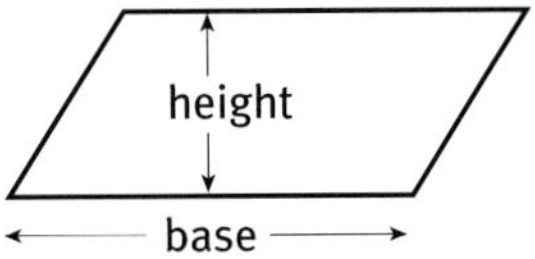

Trapezium

Area = average of parallel sides × vertical height
A = $\frac{a + b}{2} \times h$

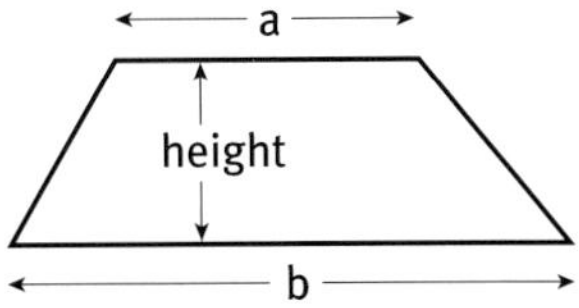

Circle

Area of circle = π × (radius)^2
A = πr^2

The **circumference** is the distance round the outside of the circle.
Circumference of circle = π × diameter
C = πd

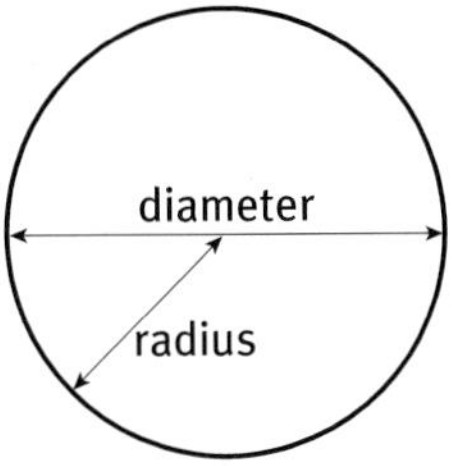

Exam tip

Remember! All your lengths must be in the same units – you can't multiply metres by centimetres!

Area under a curve

To get the approximate area under a curve, divide it up into strips, and find the total area of the strips.

- Each strip is nearly the same shape as a trapezium, and you know how to find the area of one of those.
- Find the area of all the strips and add them together to get an approximation for the area under the curve.

Find the area under the curve between 1 and 5 by dividing the area into 4 strips.

$\frac{1}{2}(1 + 1.5) \times 1 = 1.25$
$\frac{1}{2}(1.5 + 2) \times 1 = 1.75$
$\frac{1}{2}(2 + 4) \times 1 = 3$
$\frac{1}{2}(4 + 6) \times 1 = 5$
Total area $= 11$

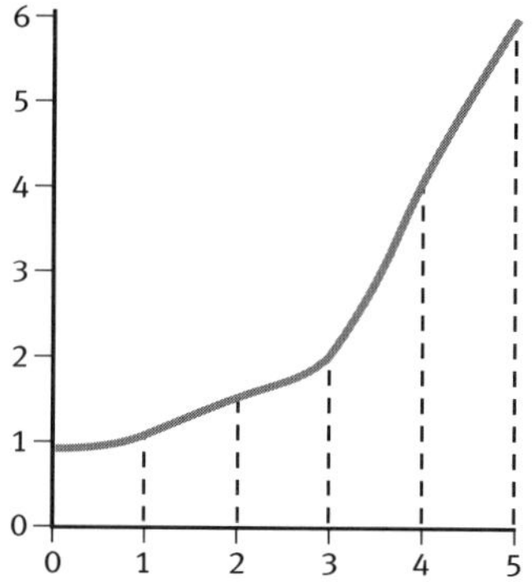

Averages

Let's look at averages using these numbers 7, 9, 5, –2, 6, 5.
The first thing to do is to rearrange them into ascending order.
So we have –2, 5, 5, 6, 7, 9

- **The Mode** is the most common value = 5
- **The Median** is the middle value, here we have two middle values so half way between them = 5.5
- **The Mean** is the $\frac{\text{total of all the items}}{\text{number of items}}$

$= \frac{-2 + 5 + 5 + 6 + 7 + 9}{6}$

$= \frac{30}{6}$

$= 5.$

Bar graph

The class names always go on the horizontal axis and the frequency is marked on the vertical axis.

- Work out the scales before you start.
- Draw the graph in pencil and use a ruler!
- Give your graph a title, for example, This is a graph to show how class 11A travel to school.

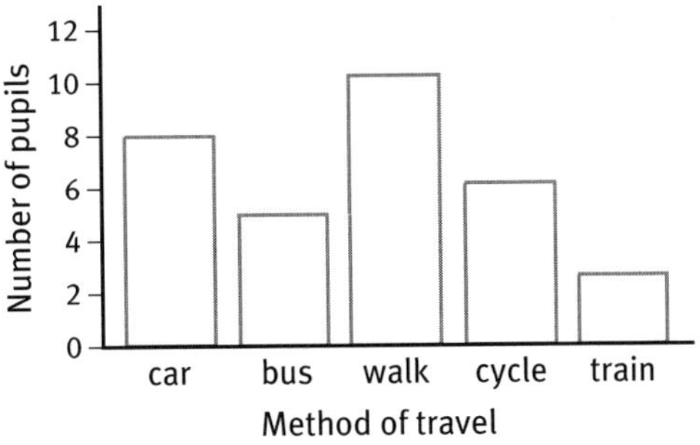

Bearings

All bearings are measured clockwise from the North line.

All bearings are written as 3 figures, e.g. 256°, 060°, 004°.

You can use what you know about angles and parallel lines to find the bearing to go back from B to A.

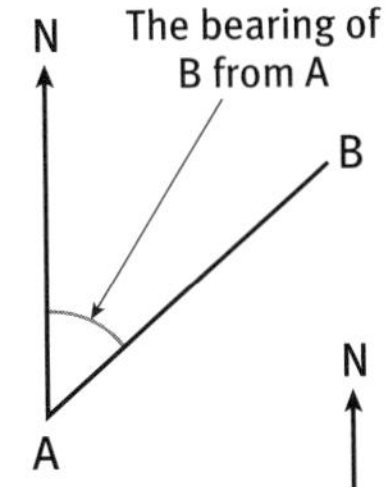

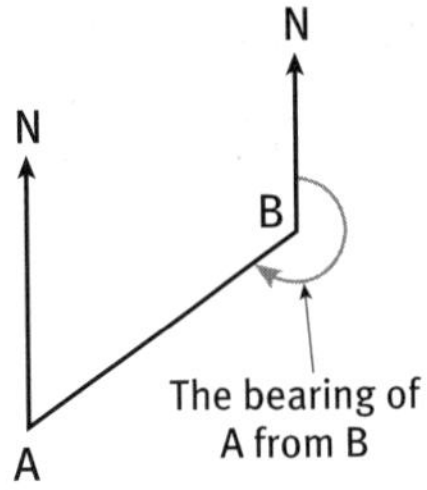

Exam tip

Always draw the North line at the point the bearing is from.

Best buy

Which is better value, 100 g of Power Brite toothpaste for £1.40 or 150 g of Glo White toothpaste for £2.70?

Find the cost for 1 g of each product.

Continued overleaf

Power Brite $\frac{140}{100} = 1.4\text{p per gram}$

Glo White $\frac{270}{150} = 1.8\text{p per gram}$

So Power Brite is better value because it costs less per gram.

Exam tip

The biggest pack is not always the best value so work it out, don't just guess!!

Bodmas

The calculator always works things out in the same order –
Brackets **O**ther **D**ivision **M**ultiplication **A**ddition **S**ubtraction

So the calculator will divide before it adds, for example, $4 + 6 \div 2$, the calculator would show the answer as 7. If you want to work things out in a different order you must remember to use brackets. The calculator will then work out what is in the brackets first so now we get $(4 + 6) \div 2 = 5$.

Brackets

- In **arithmetic**, work out what is inside the brackets first:
  $2(3 + 5) = 2 \times 8 = 16$
  $4(3^2) = 4 \times 9 = 36$
- In **algebra**, multiply out the brackets:
  $a(b + c) = ab + ac$
  Multiply out double brackets like this:

$$(2a + 4)(3a - 1) = (2a \times 3a) + (4 \times -1) + (2a \times -1) + (4 \times 3a)$$

$$= 6a^2 - 4 - 2a + 12a$$

rearrange $= 6a^2 + 10a - 4$

Exam tip

Remember: two eyebrows, a nose, and a smile!

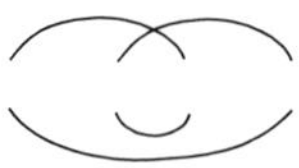

Capacity

You will need to learn these measurements for liquids.

Metric units

10 millilitres (ml) = 1 centilitre (cl)
100 centilitres = 1 litre (l)
1000 millilitres = 1 litre

Imperial units

20 fluid ounces (fl oz) = 1 pint (pt)
8 pints = 1 gallon (gal)

You should be able to convert from one set of units to the other. For example:
1 pint = 568 ml
So 4 pints = 568 × 4 = 2272 ml
Change to litres 2272 ÷ 1000 = 2.27 l

Exam tip

Remember: a litre of water's a pint and three quarters!

Completing the square

Completing the square is used to write an expression such as $a^2 + 6a + 9$ as a square number, $(a + 3)^2$.

- The number in the brackets is always half of the number in front of the a term: $\frac{1}{2} \times 6 = 3$
- Not all expressions can be written as a square number straight away: $a^2 + 6a + 10 = (a + 3)^2 + 1$
- While some expressions require you to take a number away: $a^2 + 4a = (a + 2)^2 - 4$

Exam tip

Remember to expand the brackets and check your answer if you aren't sure.

Cumulative frequency

Richard collects 40 leaves from the same bush. He measures their length to the nearest millimetre and records it in a table.

Length in cm	Frequency	Cumulative frequency
2.1 – 3	4	4
3.1 – 4	8	12
4.1 – 5	14	26
5.1 – 6	10	36
6.1 – 7	4	40

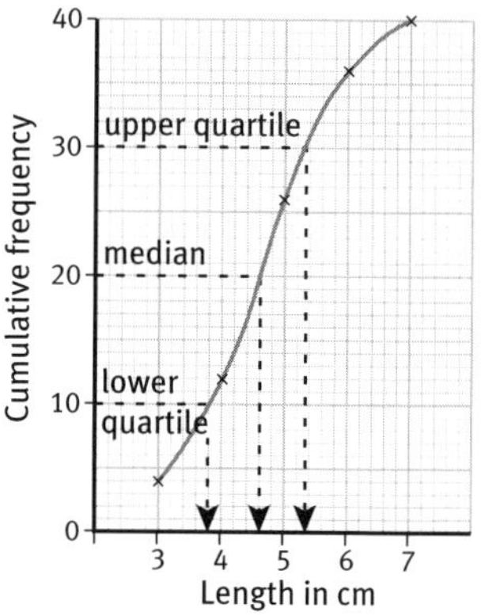

Plot the points on a graph; the horizontal axis is the upper boundary in the length column; the vertical axis is the cumulative frequency.

Join the points with a smooth curve; it should be slightly s-shaped and is unlikely to have any bumps in it!

Median mark

The line to find the median mark is drawn at $\frac{1}{2}$ the total frequency.

- Draw across at 20 until you hit the curve.
- Draw down to the length scale and read off the value.
- Median = 4.6.

Lower quartile

The line to find the lower quartile is drawn at $\frac{1}{4}$ of the total frequency.

- Lower quartile = 3.8.

Upper quartile

The line to find the upper quartile is drawn at $\frac{3}{4}$ of the total frequency.

- Upper quartile = 5.4.

Inter-quartile range

Upper quartile – lower quartile   5.4 – 3.8 = 1.6.

Cosine rule

Because the triangle is not right-angled, to find the length of side a, you must use the cosine rule:

$$a^2 = b^2 + c^2 - 2bc \cos A$$

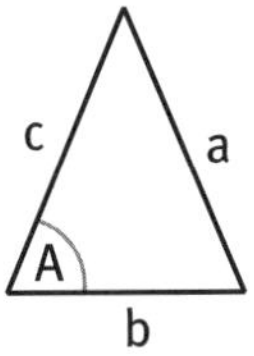

So for this triangle:

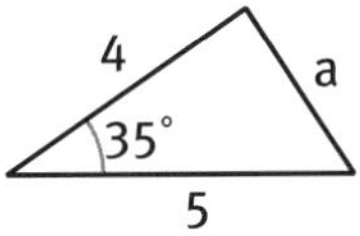

$a^2 = 5^2 + 4^2 - 2 \times 5 \times 4 \times \cos 35°$

$a = 2.87$ (2 d.p.)

Exam tip

Remember that the angle you use must be between the two sides whose length you know.

Density

Density is a measure of the mass per unit of volume, e.g. grams per cm^3

$$\textbf{Density} = \frac{\textbf{Mass}}{\textbf{Volume}}$$

This triangle will help you to get the numbers in the right place.

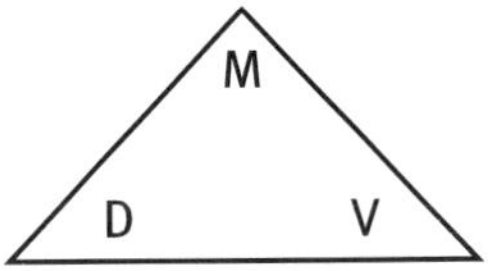

If gold has a density of 5.6 g/cm^3, a gold block of volume 50 cm^3 would have a mass of:

$50 \times 5.6 = 280$ g

Dispersion

Dispersion is a measure of how spread out a set of numbers are. There are three main types of dispersion, the range, the interquartile range, and the standard deviation (see page 35).

Range = highest value – lowest value

So for the set of numbers: 1, 2, 3, 4, 5, 6, 7, 8, 9, 10
Range = 10 – 1 = 9

Interquartile range = upper quartile – lower quartile

The upper and lower quartiles are found in a similar way to finding the median of a set of numbers:

1, 2, 3, 4, 5, 6, 7, 8, 9, 10
↑ ↑ ↑
LQ Med UQ

Median = middle value = 5.5
Upper quartile = middle value of upper half = 8
Lower quartile = middle value of lower half = 3

So the interquartile range = 8 – 3 = 5

Upper and lower quartiles can also be read from a cumulative frequency graph.

Distance, Speed and Time

The relationship between **Distance**, **Speed** and **Time** is easily remembered using this triangle.

Cover the letter you are trying to find and you have the following equations:

Distance = Speed × Time $D = S \times T$

Speed = Distance ÷ Time $S = \frac{D}{T}$

Time = Distance ÷ Speed $T = \frac{D}{S}$

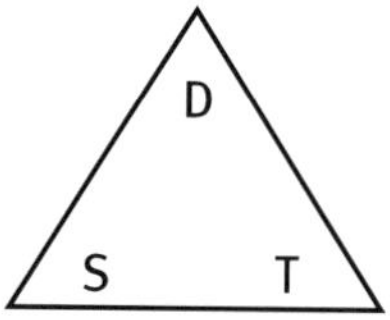

Enlargement

Enlargement, **scale factor 2**, all the sides are twice as long.

If you are given a **centre of enlargement**, use it! This will mean you get your new shape the right size and in the right place.

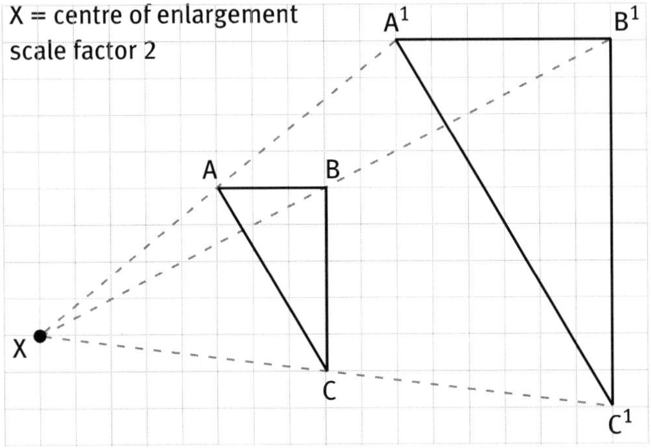

Equations

Solving equations, for example: $2t - 1.6 = 4t - 2.8$

- Add 1.6 to both sides. $2t = 4t - 1.2$
- Take 4t from both sides. $-2t = -1.2$
- Divide both sides by −2. $t = 0.6$

Always check back in the original equation:

$(2 \times 0.6) - 1.6 = (4 \times 0.6) - 2.8$

$-0.4 = -0.4$

Exam tip

Remember: you must always do the same thing to both sides of an equation to keep it balanced.

Factorisation

Example:

$4x^2 + 12x - 16 = 4\,(x^2 + 3x - 4)$
Multiply out to check
$4\,(x^2 + 3x - 4) = 4x^2 + 12x - 16$

Foreign currency

The **exchange rate** is the value of a **single unit** of **currency.**

For Belgian Francs, the exchange rate is £1 = 63 BEF.

To change £ to BEF, multiply by 63.

To change BEF to £, divide by 63.

For example: to change £58 to BEF: $58 \times 63 = 3654$ BEF

to change 650 BEF to £: $650 \div 63 = £10.32$

Fractional equations

Example: $\frac{1}{x} + 2 = 4$

- Multiply both sides by x — $1 + 2x = 4x$
- Take $2x$ from both sides — $1 = 2x$
- Divide both sides by 2 — $x = \frac{1}{2}$

A harder equation: $\frac{x}{4} + \frac{3}{x} = 2$

- Combine fractions — $\frac{x^2 + 12}{4x} = 2$
- Multiply both sides by $4x$ — $x^2 + 12 = 8x$
- Take $8x$ from both sides — $x^2 - 8x + 12 = 0$
- Factorise — $(x - 2)\,(x - 6) = 0$

$x = 2$ or $x = 6$

Cancelling fractions

Divide top and bottom by the same number.

$\frac{8}{10} = \frac{4}{5}$ $\frac{24}{36} = \frac{2}{3}$

Mixed numbers ↔ improper fractions

$1\frac{3}{4} = \frac{7}{4}$ $(1 \times 4) + 3 = 7$

$\frac{14}{3} = 4\frac{2}{3}$ $14 \div 3 = 4 \text{ r } 2$

The four rules – one example of each just to refresh your memory. You may need to do these without a calculator!

Addition

$$3\frac{1}{2} + 2\frac{2}{3} = 5\frac{1}{2} + \frac{2}{3}$$

find lowest common denominator

$$= 5\frac{3+4}{6}$$

$$= 5\frac{7}{6}$$

$$= 5 + 1\frac{1}{6}$$

$$= 6\frac{1}{6}$$

Subtraction

Very similar to addition.

$$3\frac{1}{2} - 1\frac{3}{5} = 2\frac{1}{2} - \frac{3}{5}$$

$$= 2\frac{5-6}{10}$$

$$= 2 - \frac{1}{10}$$

$$= 1\frac{9}{10}$$

Multiplication

$$1\frac{1}{2} \times \frac{3}{5} = \frac{3}{2} \times \frac{3}{5}$$

$$= \frac{9}{10}$$

Division

Very similar to multiplication.

$$2\frac{1}{2} \div \frac{3}{5} = \frac{5}{2} \div \frac{3}{5}$$

$$= \frac{5}{2} \times \frac{5}{3}$$

$$= \frac{25}{6}$$

$$= 4\frac{1}{6}$$

Frequency polygon

The easiest way to show how a frequency polygon is drawn is to put it over the top of a histogram.

For example:

- put a dot at the top of each bar in the centre
- join the dots with a ruler
- do not join to the axes.

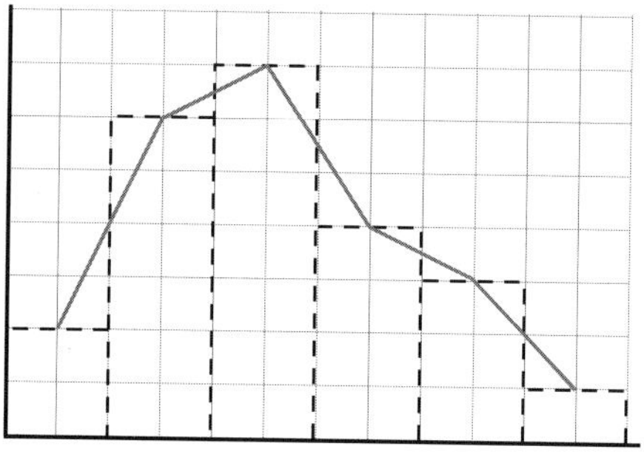

Gradient of a curve

To find the gradient of a point on a curve, draw the tangent at the point, then find the gradient of the tangent.

For example:
find the gradient at the point (2, 4).

- First, draw the tangent at (2, 4).
- Choose two points on the tangent, for instance (1, 0) and (3, 8).
- Find the gradient of the tangent: $\frac{8-0}{3-1} = 4$
- So the gradient of the curve at the point (2, 4) is 4.

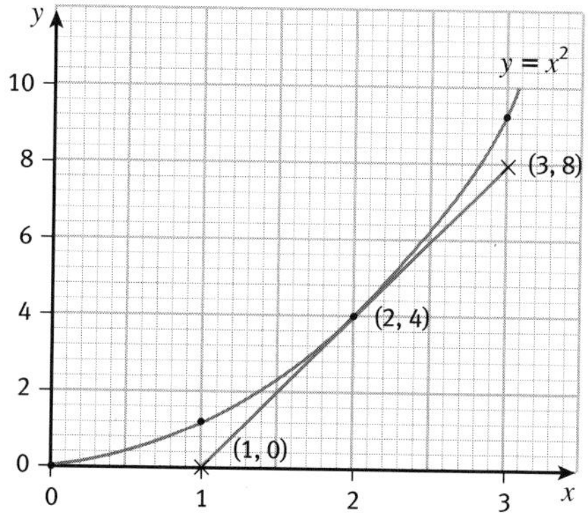

Exam tip

Remember to get the values the correct way round when working out the gradient.

Gradient of a straight line

You can use the same method for finding the gradient of a straight line as you use for finding the gradient of the tangent to a curve. (See the previous entry.) If the gradient of the graph is in the form $y = mx + c$, the gradient is given by the value of m. The point where the line crosses the y axis is given by c.

Highest common factor

The highest common factor, **HCF**, is the largest factor which will divide exactly into 2 numbers.

- First write the numbers as products of their prime factors.

2	48	2	540
2	24	2	270
2	12	3	135
2	6	3	45
3	3	3	15
	1	5	5
			1

- Circle the numbers they have in common.

  ② × ② × 2 × 2 × ③ ② × ② × ③ × 3 × 3 × 5
- The HCF is then $2 \times 2 \times 3 = 12$.

Index notation

4^3 4 to the power 3 = $4 \times 4 \times 4$
5^6 5 to the power 6 = $5 \times 5 \times 5 \times 5 \times 5 \times 5$

- When **multiplying** with indices you **add** the powers.

  So $5^2 \times 5^3 = 5^{2+3} = 5^5$

  Similarly with negative numbers

  $5^{-2} \times 5^3 = 5^{-2+3} = 5^1$

Continued overleaf

- When **dividing** with indices you **subtract** the powers.
  So, $6^5 \div 6^3 = 6^{5-3} = 6^2$ and $6^{-2} \div 6^3 = 6^{-2-3} = 6^{-5}$

Anything to the power 1 is itself $2^1 = 2$
Anything to the power 0 is 1 $4^0 = 1$

Inequalities

Solving inequalities is very similar to solving normal equations.

For example: $3 - 5x < 2x + 17$

- Add $5x$ to both sides $3 < 7x + 17$
- Take 17 from both sides $-14 < 7x$
- Divide both sides by 7 $-2 < x$

The main difference in solving inequalities when compared to normal equations is that if you multiply or divide by a negative number, you must reverse the inequality.

A simple example of this:

$-\frac{x}{2} > 8$ Multiply both sides by –2 and reverse the inequality

$x < -16$

Length

Metric units

10 millimetres (mm) = 1 centimetre (cm)
100 centimetres = 1 metre (m)
1000 metres = 1 kilometre (km)

Imperial units

12 inches (in) = 1 foot (ft)
3 feet = 1 yard (yd)
1760 yards = 1 mile

You should be able to convert from one set of units to the other.
For example: 1 inch = 2.5 centimetres

so 12 inches = $2.5 \times 12 = 30$ centimetres (length of a ruler).

Linear inequalities

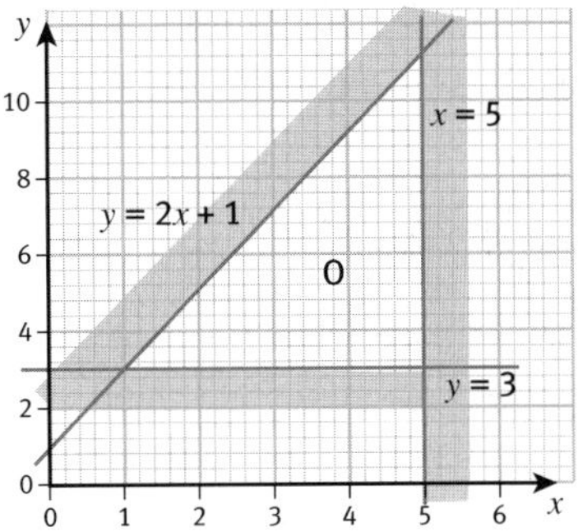

Plotting lines on a graph and finding a region where all the points satisfy a set of inequalities. For example:

$x < 5$ read as x is less than 5

$y > 3$ read as y is greater than 3

$y < 2x + 1$ read as y is less than $2x + 1$

Onto a graph you need to draw the lines:

$x = 5$ $y = 3$ $y = 2x + 1$

One side of each line satisfies the inequality. If you **shade** the side of the line that you don't want, you will be left with an unshaded region which fits all the inequalities.

To check: pick a point inside the region and make sure it fits all the requirements.

$(x, y) = (4, 6)$ $x < 5$ yes

$y > 3$ yes

$y < 2x + 1$ $6 < 9$ Yes

Line graph

The temperature in a classroom was recorded every three hours and the results plotted on a line graph.

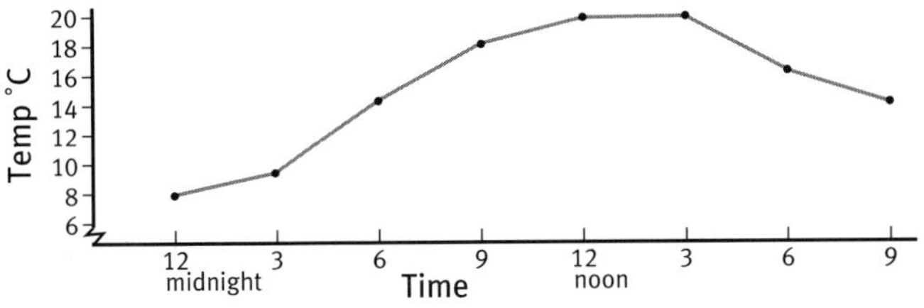

As each point is plotted it is joined to the previous point with a straight line. (Use a ruler!)

Exam tip

Note the symbol used to show that the vertical axis does not start at 0.

Line of best fit

This is the line you are usually asked to draw on a **scatter diagram**.

You have to decide where to put the line. Try to get an equal number of crosses on either side of your line.

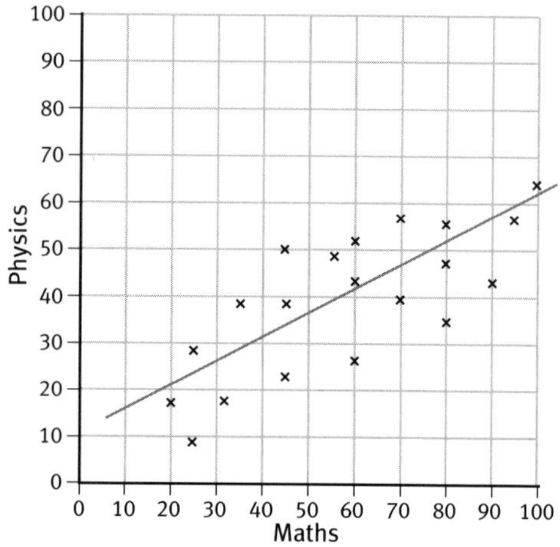

This line can now be used to **estimate** a mark for a pupil who scored 60 for the maths test but was absent for the physics. Find 60 on the axis for maths, go up until you hit the line and then read across for the physics mark.

As you can see, the marks for maths were generally better than those for physics!

Locus

The locus of a point is the **path** which it **makes** as it **moves**.

The locus of a point a **fixed distance** (x units) from **point A** is a circle.

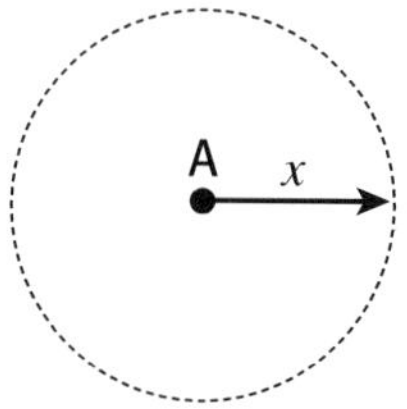

The locus of a point a fixed distance (x units) from the **line AB** is a pair of parallel lines.

The locus of a point equidistant from **2 points A and B** is the perpendicular bisector of AB.

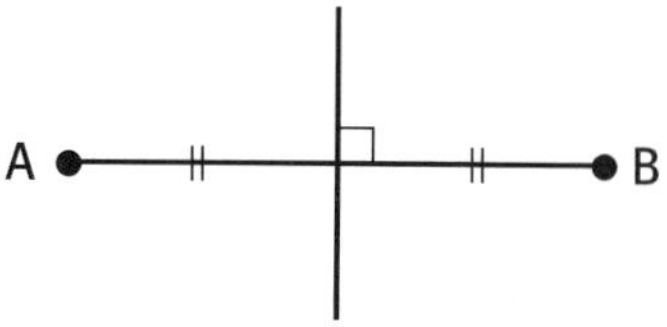

The locus of a point equidistant from **2 lines AB and AC** is the line which bisects ∠ BAC.

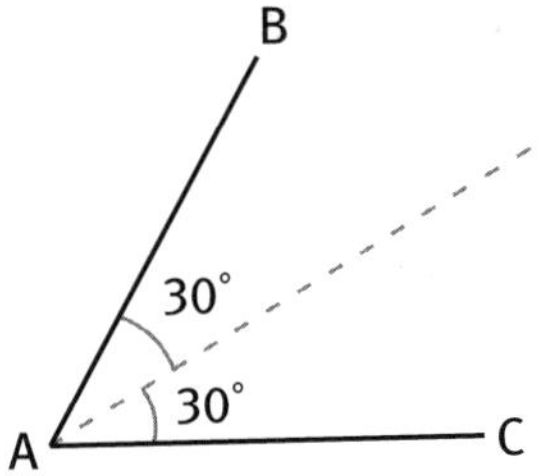

Lowest common multiple

The lowest common multiple, **LCM,** is the lowest number which 2 numbers will divide into exactly.

To find the LCM of 24 and 16.

- First write the numbers as products of their prime factors.

2	24	2	16
2	12	2	8
2	6	2	4
3	3	2	2
	1		1

- Circle the numbers they have in common.

② × ② × ② × 3   ② × ② × ② × 2

- The LCM is then $2 \times 2 \times 2 \times 2 \times 3 = 48$

Use all the numbers from the first set and the numbers that are **not** circled from the second set.

Multiples

The answers in the 7 times table are all multiples of 7: 14, 21, 28, 35, 42 . . .

100 is a multiple of 20, because $20 \times 5 = 100$

72 is a multiple of 9, because $9 \times 8 = 72$

Negative numbers

Multiplying and dividing

$(+4) \times (+3) = +12$
$(-4) \times (-3) = +12$
$\dfrac{(+12)}{(+4)} = +3$
$\dfrac{(-12)}{(-4)} = +3$

If the **signs** are the **same**, the answer is **positive**.

$(-4) \times (+3) = -12$
$(+4) \times (-3) = -12$
$\dfrac{(+12)}{(-4)} = -3$
$\dfrac{(-12)}{(+4)} = -3$

If the **signs** are **different**, the answer is **negative**.

Adding and subtracting

You can use a **number line** for counting **up**, when the sign is **positive**, and **down**, when the sign is **negative**.

$4 - 3 = +1$ $\quad (-3) + 6 = +3$
$4 - 6 = -2$ $\quad (-3) + 1 = -2$

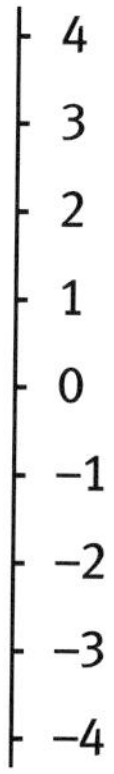

If you have 2 signs next to each other they should be replaced with one sign. You can then use the number line to work out the answer.

$5 + (+7) = 5 + 7 = 12$
$5 - (-7) = 5 + 7 = 12$

If the signs are the **same**, replace with a **+**.

$5 + (-7) = 5 - 7 = -2$
$5 - (+7) = 5 - 7 = -2$

If the signs are **different**, replace with a **–**.

Exam tip

It is worth doing some extra practice with negative numbers, a slip up here can cause a lot of problems with algebra!

A number pattern or sequence is a list of numbers where there is a relationship between each number, for instance:

1, 3, 5, 7, 9, 11 . . .

This number pattern is found by adding 2 to the previous term.

There are several important number patterns.

- Square numbers:
  1, 4, 9, 16, 25 . . .
- Triangular numbers:
  1, 3, 6, 10, 15 . . .
- The Fibonacci sequence, which is found by adding the last two numbers together:
  1, 1, 2, 3, 5, 8, 13, 21, 34 . . .

Linear patterns are those where each term has a common difference, like the first example. To find the *n*th term of a linear sequence (which is often called U_n), use the rule:

$$U_n = an + b$$

where a is the common difference, and b is found by substituting in the first term of the sequence.

For example:
find the 10th term of the sequence:
2, 5, 8, 11, 14 . . .

- Find the common difference, $5 - 2 = 3$
- Find b by entering in the first term, i.e. $n = 1$
  $2 = 3 \times 1 + b$
  $b = -1$
- So the final rule for this sequence is $U_n = 3n - 1$
- The 10th term $= 3 \times 10 - 1 = 29$.

Percentage error

Percentage error is a measure of how accurate an estimated answer is.

For example:
find the area of a rectangle with sides of length 2.12 cm and 5.96 cm.

- To make it easier to calculate, round the lengths to the nearest cm, and work out an estimated area:
  $2 \times 6 = 12 \text{ cm}^2$
- Later on, work out the area accurately:
  $2.12 \times 5.96 = 12.6352 \text{ cm}^2$

To find the percentage error you made in your estimate:

- first find the difference between the two answers
- then divide this by the correct answer
- finally multiply this by 100 to get a percentage.

$$\textbf{Percentage error} = \frac{\textbf{estimated value} - \textbf{true value}}{\textbf{true value}} \times 100$$

So in this case, your percentage error was:

$$\frac{12 - 12.6352}{12.6352} \times 100 = 5.03\% \text{ (2 d.p.)}$$

If the error comes out as **negative**, you can **ignore** this and **write** it as **positive**, as you only want to know how far out an estimate was, not whether it was more or less than the correct answer.

Percentages

To find a percentage of a quantity

$35\% \text{ of } £5 = \frac{35}{100} \times 5 = £1.75$

To increase by a percentage

Find the new price if £9.00 is increased by 25%.

$25\% \text{ of } £9 = \frac{25}{100} \times 9 = £2.25$

New price = £9 + £2.25 = £11.25

To decrease by a percentage

Find the new price if £9.00 is decreased by 15%

$15\% \text{ of } £9 = \frac{15}{100} \times 9 = £1.35$

New price = £9 – £1.35 = £7.65

To express one quantity as a percentage of another

In a Maths test you get 45 marks out of 60!

As a percentage this is $\frac{45}{60} \times 100 = 75\%$

To find a percentage increase or decrease

The price of a car is increased from £7950 to £8400. Find the percentage increase.

Difference in price = £8400 – £7950 = £450

$\text{Percentage change} = \frac{\text{difference in price}}{\text{original price}} = \frac{450}{7950} \times 100 = 5.7\%$

Exam tip

You may need to answer percentage questions without a calculator!

Pie charts

30 students are asked what they had for breakfast this morning.

Cereal	8	Toast	9	Bacon and egg	4
Drink only	7	Nothing	2		

Set this information out in a table so that you can work out the angles for the pie chart. There are 360° altogether and 30 students, $360° \div 30 = 12°$ per student.

Breakfast	No. of students	Angle
Cereal	8	96°
Toast	9	108°
Bacon and egg	4	48°
Drink only	7	84°
Nothing	2	24°
Totals	30	360°

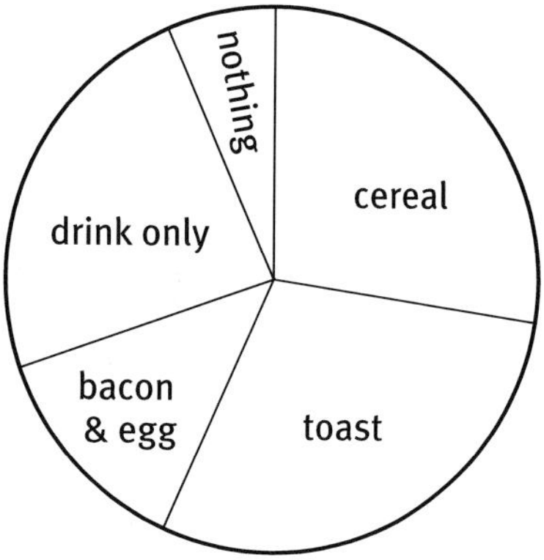

Now you are ready to draw the pie chart, in pencil, not too small.
Measure each angle carefully and label the sectors.

Polygons

A polygon is a many sided figure. A **regular polygon** has all its sides the same length.

Here are the names for some polygons.

Name	Number of sides	Name	Number of sides
triangle	3	heptagon	7
quadrilateral	4	octagon	8
pentagon	5	nonagon	9
hexagon	6	decagon	10

Probability

The probability of anything happening lies somewhere between 0 and 1, impossible and certain. So answers of 1.6 or $2\frac{1}{2}$ are definitely wrong!

The 'and' rule

- The probability that it will rain tomorrow is $\frac{1}{4}$.
- The probability that I will have toast for breakfast tomorrow is $\frac{1}{2}$.
- The probability that it will rain tomorrow **and** I will have toast for breakfast is: $\frac{1}{4} \times \frac{1}{2} = \frac{1}{8}$.

The 'or' rule

A box contains 20 chocolates: 8 are milk chocolates, 5 plain chocolates and the other 7 are white chocolates. If I close my eyes and pick a chocolate, the probability of it being milk **or** white is:

$$\frac{8}{20} + \frac{7}{20} = \frac{15}{20} = \frac{3}{4}$$

Proportionality

If two variables are in **direct proportion**, then as one **increases or decreases,** the other does the **same**. Variables in direct proportion can be written where one variable equals the other, multiplied by a constant.

$$\mathbf{Y \propto X}$$
$$\mathbf{Y = kX}$$

Inverse proportion is where as one variable **increases,** the other **decreases,** and **vice versa**. Similarly, inverse proportion can be written using a constant.

$$\mathbf{Y \propto \frac{1}{X}}$$
$$\mathbf{Y = \frac{k}{X}}$$

Pythagoras' theorem

This is only for use with right-angled triangles when we know the length of two sides and need to find the third.

$$c^2 = a^2 + b^2$$

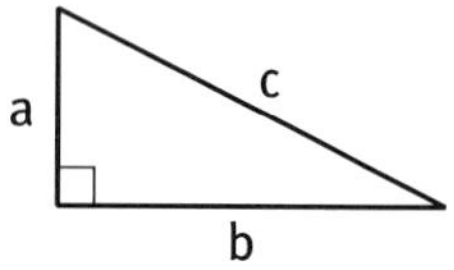

c is the **hypotenuse**, the longest side, opposite the right angle.

For example: to find the length PX

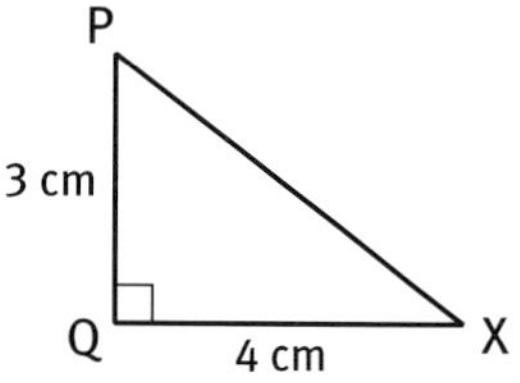

$$\begin{aligned} c^2 &= a^2 + b^2 \\ &= 4^2 + 3^2 \\ &= 16 + 9 \\ &= 25 \\ c &= \sqrt{25} \\ c &= 5 \text{ cm} \end{aligned}$$

Quadratic equations

Some quadratic equations can be solved by factorising the equation, but there are many that cannot be solved easily using this method. Instead of factorising, you must use the quadratic formula:

if $ax^2 + bx + c = 0$, then $x = \dfrac{-b \pm \sqrt{b^2 - 4ac}}{2a}$

For example: $x^2 + 3x + 1 = 0$

This equation cannot easily be factorised, so use the formula:

$$x = \frac{-3 \pm \sqrt{3^2 - 4 \times 1 \times 1}}{2 \times 1}$$

$$x = \frac{-3 \pm \sqrt{5}}{2}$$

There are two possible answers:

1. $x = \dfrac{-3 + \sqrt{5}}{2} = -0.38$ (2 d.p.)

2. $x = \dfrac{-3 - \sqrt{5}}{2} = -2.62$ (2 d.p.)

So $x = -0.38$, or $x = -2.62$

Quadratic graphs

These are graphs with x^2 in them. They are always curves. You will be given an equation and a range of values for x.

For example:
$y = x^2 - 3$ for $-4 \leqslant x \leqslant +4$

Make a table for the range of x values, and fill it in.

x	−4	−3	−2	−1	0	1	2	3	4
x^2	16	9	4	1	0	1	4	9	16
−3	−3	−3	−3	−3	−3	−3	−3	−3	−3
y	13	6	1	−2	−3	−2	1	6	13

- To draw the graph, we need:
  x values from −4 to +4
  y values from −3 to +13.
- In pencil, draw the axes and label them x and y.
- Plot the points and join them with a smooth curve.

Your curve should be symmetrical: check your values if it has any strange wiggles!

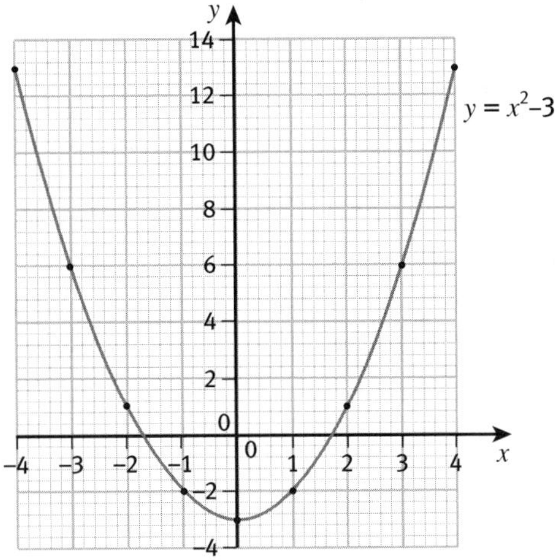

Exam tip

It is sometimes easier to draw the curve if you turn the paper upside down!

Quadrilaterals

Quad means 4. So quadrilaterals are 4-sided figures. Here are some facts you should know about common quadrilaterals. For **all** of them, the **interior angles** add up to **360°**.

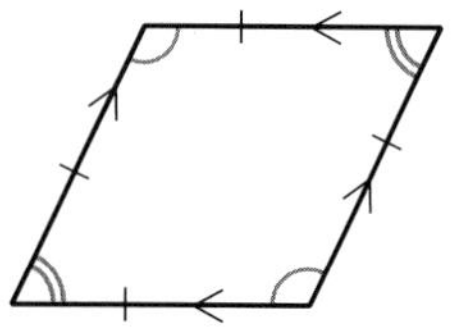

Rhombus

- 4 equal sides
- 2 pairs of parallel sides
- opposite angles equal

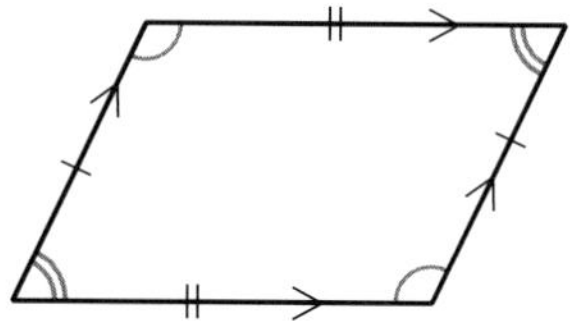

Parallelogram

- opposite sides equal
- 2 pairs of parallel sides
- opposite angles equal

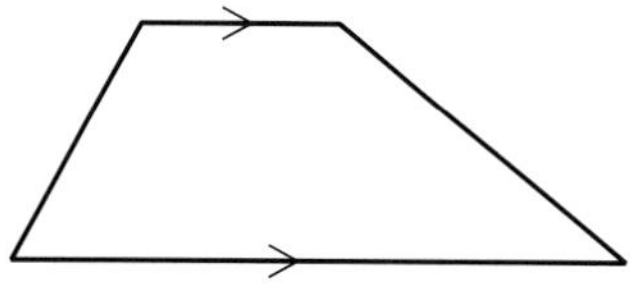

Trapezium

- no equal sides
- 1 pair parallel sides
- no equal angles

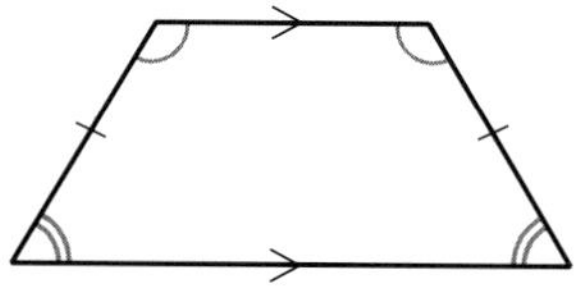

Isosceles Trapezium

- 2 equal sides
- 1 pair parallel sides
- 2 pairs equal angles

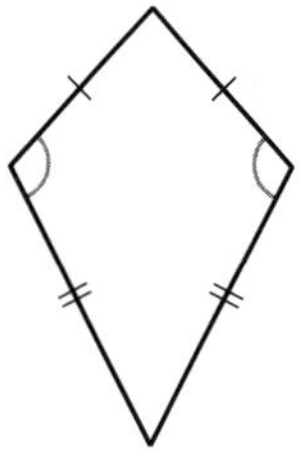

Kite

- 2 pairs equal sides
- no parallel sides
- 1 pair equal angles

You can also look at the diagonals of these figures.

- Do they bisect each other?
- Do they cross at right-angles?

Rational numbers

Rational numbers include integers, fractions and mixed numbers.

Fractions that can be written as exact decimals,

$\frac{3}{4} = 0.75$

or as decimals with a recurring pattern,

$\frac{1}{3} = 0.33333\ldots = 0.\dot{3}$

are rational numbers.

Rearranging formulae

Make x the subject of the following equation:
$y = 3x - 4xz + 12y - 2$

- Collect all x on one side $\quad 2 - 11y = 3x - 4xz$
- Factorise $\quad 2 - 11y = x(3 - 4z)$
- Divide both sides by $(3 - 4z)$ $\quad x = \frac{2 - 11y}{3 - 4z}$

Now make x the subject of this equation:
$x + \frac{y^2}{x} = \frac{yz}{x} - 2y$

- Multiply both sides by x $\quad x^2 + y^2 = yz - 2yx$
- Collect all x on one side $\quad x^2 + 2xy + y^2 = yz$
- Factorise $\quad (x + y)^2 = yz$
- Take the square root of both sides $\quad x + y = \sqrt{yz}$
- Take y from both sides $\quad x = \sqrt{yz} - y$

Reflections

Here is one of your favourite words reflected in the mirror line AB!

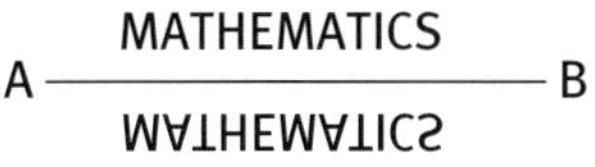

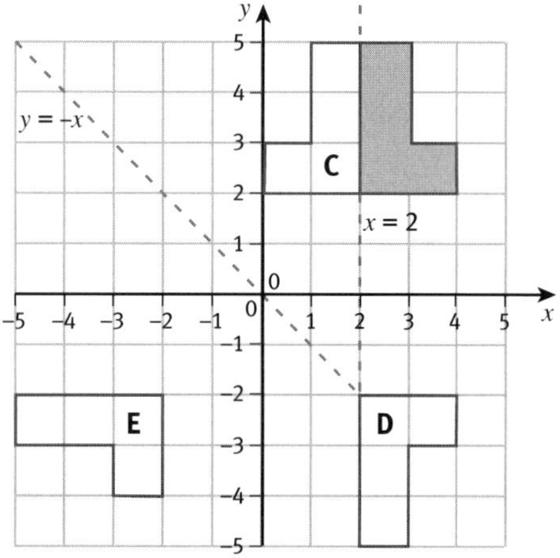

The size and shape of the letters is not altered. The original word and its reflection are both the same distance away from the mirror line.

- C is a reflection of the shaded figure in the line $x = 2$.
- D is a reflection of the shaded figure in the x axis.
- E is a reflection of the shaded figure in the line $y = -x$.
- The mirror line is called the **axis of reflection.**

Rotational symmetry

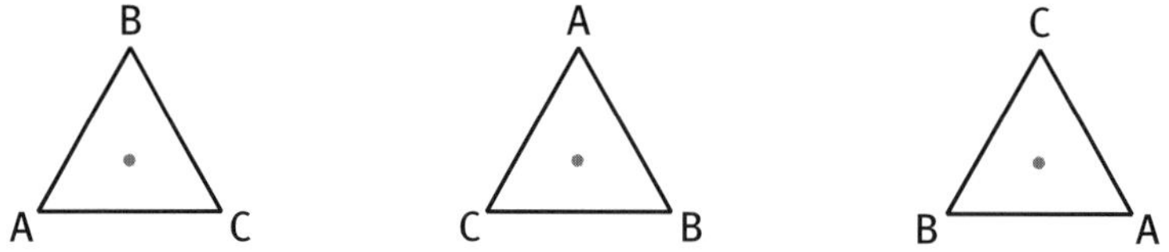

An equilateral triangle has rotational symmetry order 3. As it turns through 360° there are 3 positions it can stop and look the same.

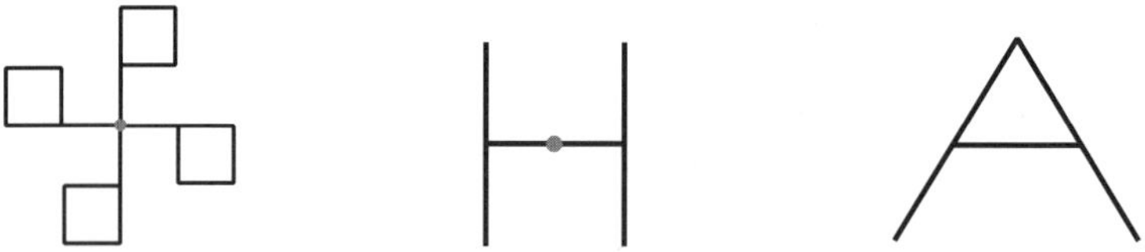

Rotational symmetry order 4.

Rotational symmetry order 2.

Rotational symmetry order 1.

Rotations

To turn a figure through an angle about a fixed point is called a rotation. The fixed point is called the **centre of rotation**. The size and shape of the figure stay the same.

- If the shaded figure is rotated 90° clockwise about (0, 0), the result will be figure A.
- If the shaded figure is rotated 180° about (–1, 2), the result will be figure B.

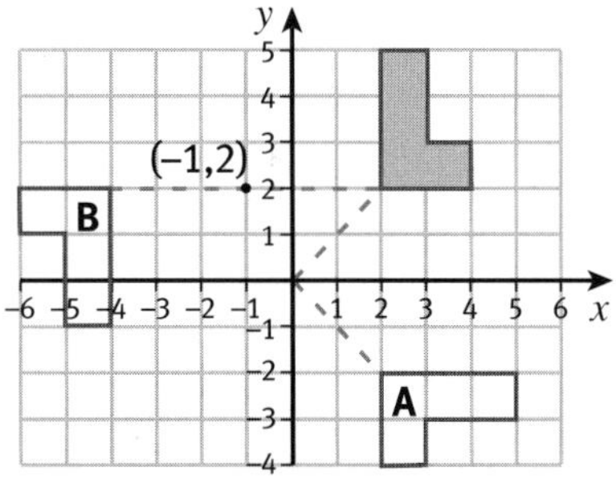

Sample space diagrams

This shows all the possible outcomes when two events occur. If 2 dice are thrown and the scores are added the diagram would look like this:

	Blue Die					
+	1	2	3	4	5	6
1	2	3	4	5	6	7
2	3	4	5	6	7	8
3	4	5	6	7	8	9
4	5	6	7	8	9	10
5	6	7	8	9	10	11
6	7	8	9	10	11	12

There are 36 possible outcomes. You can now work out the probability of any particular score.

P (5) $= \frac{4}{36} = \frac{1}{9}$ P (10 or more) $= \frac{6}{36} = \frac{1}{6}$

Scatter diagrams

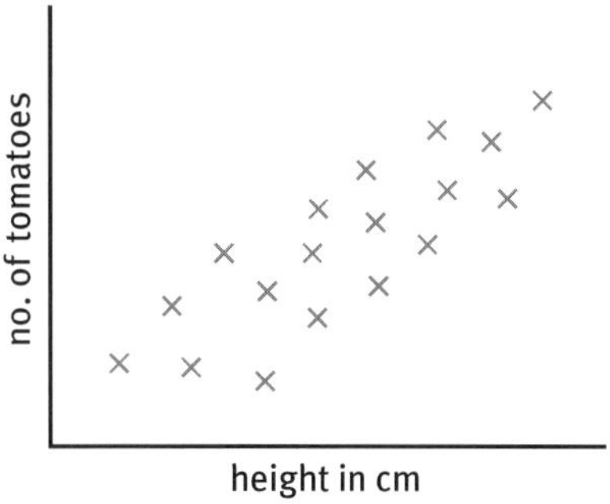

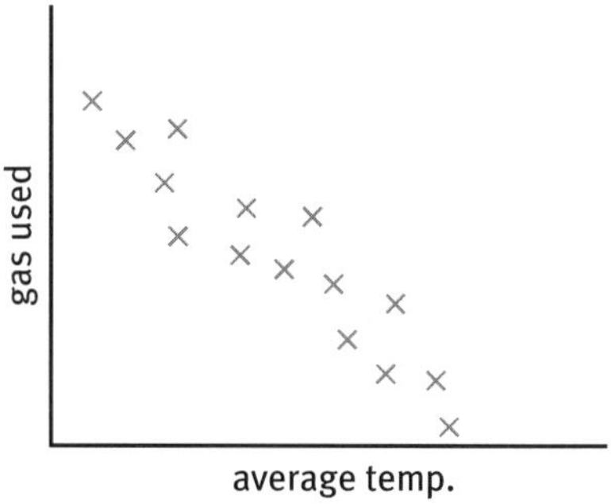

There is a **positive correlation** between the height of a tomato plant and the number of tomatoes on the plant. Taller plants tend to have more tomatoes.

There is a **negative correlation** between the average daily temperature and the number of therms of gas used for heating. The higher the temperature, the lower the gas consumption.

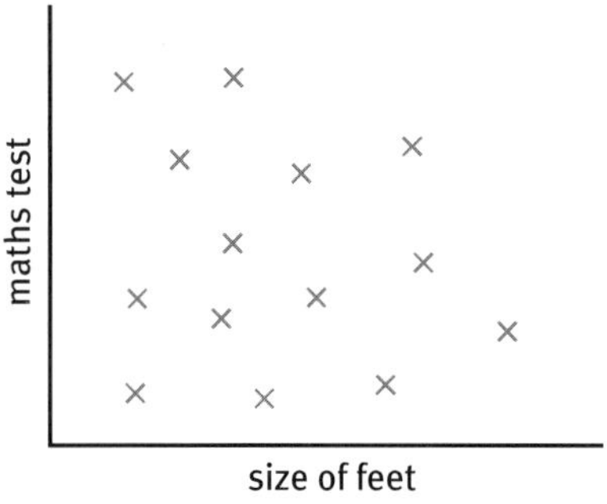

There is **no correlation** between the size of your feet and your ability to do well in a maths test!

Exam tip

The closer the points are to forming a straight line, the stronger the correlation. If the points are scattered, there is no correlation.

Sectors and segments

Area of a sector = $\frac{a}{360^\circ} \times \pi r^2$

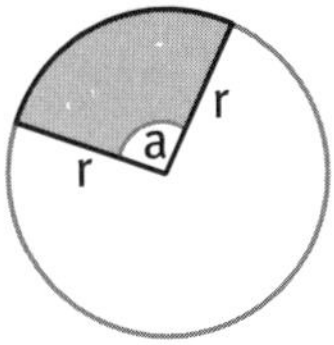

The area of a segment is the area of the sector minus the area of the triangle made with the chord and the radii.

Area of segment = $\frac{a}{360^\circ} \times \pi r^2 - \frac{1}{2} r^2 \times \sin a$

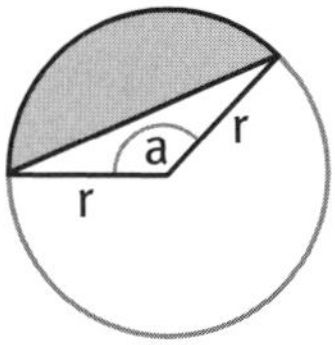

Significant figures

Use the same rules as for decimal places: if the next figure is 5 or more, round the number up.

43.5064 has 6 significant figures.
If we reduce it to 3 significant figures (s.f.) we get:

43.5

0.00365 has 3 significant figures.
If we reduce it to 2 s.f. we get:

0.0037

The first significant figure is the first figure which is not 0.

Exam tip

The numbers must all keep their original place value.
6375 = 6400 to 2 s.f. not 64!

Simultaneous equations

This is where you have 2 equations each with 2 letters in them. You need to find solutions that fit both equations. For example:

$2x + 3y = 1$
$4y - 3x = -10$

To find x and y, first rearrange the terms so they are in the same order

$2x + 3y = 1$ call this equation ①
$-3x + 4y = -10$ and this equation ②

To eliminate x, multiply equation ① by 3 and equation ② by 2. This will give $6x$ in both equations:

$6x + 9y = 3$
$-6x + 8y = -20$

Add equations together (if $6x$ was positive in both equations you would need to subtract):

$17y = -17$
$y = -1$

To find x, substitute $y = -1$ in equation ①

$2x + 3(-1) = 1$
$2x - 3 = 1$
$2x - 3 + 3 = 1 + 3$
$2x = 4$
$x = 2$

Check your answers in equation ②

$x = 2 \quad y = -1$
$4y - 3x = -4 - 6 = -10$

Exam tip

The check at the end will confirm if you have the right solutions. If it doesn't work – try again!

Sine rule

Because the triangle is not right-angled, to find the angle A you must use the sine rule:

$$\frac{\mathbf{a}}{\mathbf{\sin A}} = \frac{\mathbf{b}}{\mathbf{\sin B}}$$

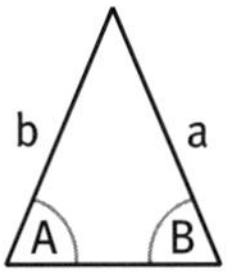

So for this triangle:

$$\frac{5}{\sin 40} = \frac{6}{\sin B}$$

$$\sin B = \frac{6 \times \sin 40}{5}$$

$B = 50.47^{\circ}$ (2 d.p.)

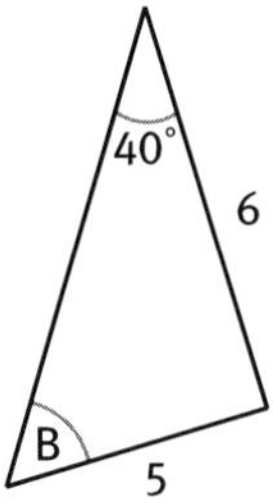

Standard deviation

This is a method of measuring **dispersion**. In a given set of numbers the standard deviation measures how far away the numbers are from the mean. The standard deviation can be written in two ways; the second is better if the mean is not exact.

$$\textbf{Standard deviation} = \sqrt{\frac{\Sigma (x - \bar{x})^2}{n}} = \sqrt{\frac{\Sigma x^2}{n} - \bar{x}^2}$$

Find the mean and standard deviation of the following set of numbers:
15, 16, 17, 17, 19, 24

- First find the mean: $\frac{15 + 16 + 17 + 17 + 19 + 24}{6} = 18$
- Square the difference between each number and the mean:

  $(18 - 15)^2 = 9$

  $(18 - 16)^2 = 4$

  $(18 - 17)^2 = 1$

  $(18 - 17)^2 = 1$

  $(18 - 19)^2 = 1$

  $(18 - 24)^2 = 36$

Continued overleaf

- Add the squares together, and find their average:
  $\frac{9+4+1+1+1+36}{6} = 8.67$ (2 d.p.)
- The standard deviation is the square root of this value
  $\sqrt{8.67} = 2.94$ (2 d.p.)

Standard form

This is used for writing very large or very small numbers.
$4.68 \times 10^{6} = 4\,680\,000$
$4.68 \times 10^{-6} = 0.00000468$

To remind you how it works:
4.68×10^{2} is the same as $4.68 \times 10 \times 10$.

For 10^{2}, move all the numbers 2 places to the left:

Th	H	T	U	·	$\frac{1}{10}$	$\frac{1}{100}$	
			4	·	6	8	× 10 gives:
		4	6	·	8		× 10 gives:
	4	6	8				

So $4.68 \times 10^{2} = 468$

For 10^{4}, you would move all numbers 4 places to the left.

So $4.68 \times 10^{4} = 46\,800$

For 4.68×10^{-2}, move all the numbers 2 places to the right:

U	·	$\frac{1}{10}$	$\frac{1}{100}$	$\frac{1}{1000}$	$\frac{1}{10000}$
4	·	6	8		
0	·	4	6	8	
0	·	0	4	6	8

So $4.68 \times 10^{-2} = 0.0468$

Substitution in algebra

Substitution is where you put number values instead of the letters in an equation, and work out the answer.

For example:
find w if $x = -4$, $y = 3$ and $z = 2$

$w = 2x + y - 3z$
$w = (2 \times -4) + 3 - (3 \times 2)$
$= -8 + 3 - 6$
$= -11$
so $w = -11$

Exam tip

Be careful with the + and – signs.

Surface area

- Surface area of a **prism**.
  We have 2 identical triangles and 3 rectangles.

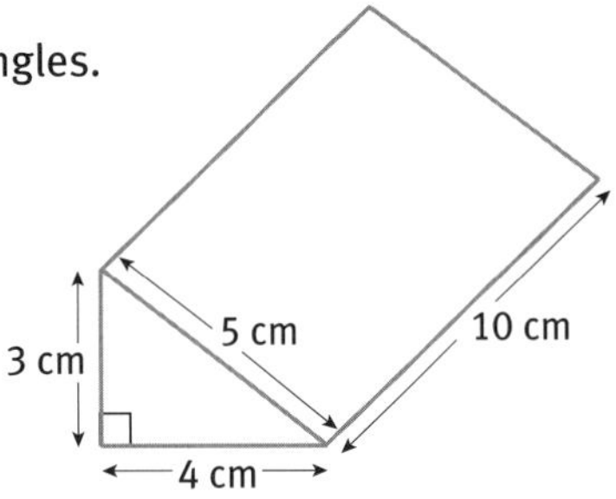

Area of 1 triangle	$= \frac{4 \times 3}{2}$ =	6
Area of 2 triangles	$= 2 \times 6$ =	12
Back rectangle	$= 3 \times 10$ =	30
Base rectangle	$= 4 \times 10$ =	40
Front rectangle	$= 5 \times 10$ =	50
Total surface area		$= 132\ cm^2$

- Surface area of a **cylinder**.
  We have 2 circles and the curved surface. This opens out into a rectangle: the width is the height of the cylinder and the length is the circumference of the circle.

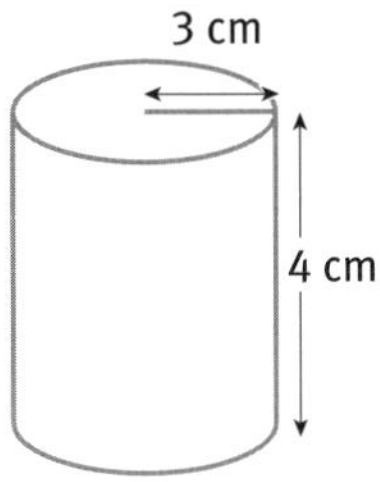

Area of 2 circles $= 2(\pi r^2) = 2 \times \pi \times r^2$
$= 2 \times \pi \times 3^2 = 56.55\ cm^2$

Area of curved surface
$= 2\pi rh = 2 \times \pi \times r \times h$
$= 2 \times \pi \times 3 \times 4 = 75.40\ cm^2$

Total surface area = $131.95\ cm^2$

Continued overleaf

- Surface area of a **cone**.
  We have 1 circle and the curved surface. The length of the slant is called L (5 cm) and the radius of the circle is 2 cm.

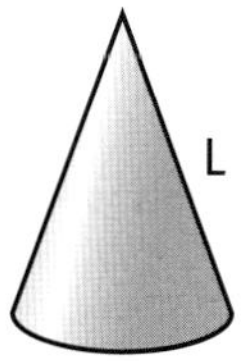

Area of circle $= (\boldsymbol{\pi r^2})$
$= \pi \times r^2$
$= \pi \times 2^2 = 12.57$

Area of curved surface $= \boldsymbol{\pi rL}$
$= \pi \times r \times L$
$= \pi \times 2 \times 5 = 31.42$

Total surface area = 43.99 cm^2

- Surface area of a **sphere**.

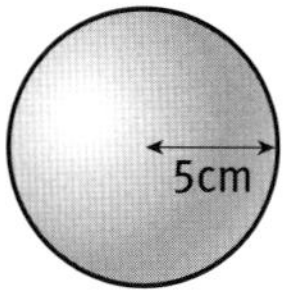

Area of sphere $= \boldsymbol{4\ (\pi r^2)}$
$= 4 \times \pi \times r^2$
$= 4 \times \pi \times 5^2$
$= 314.16\ cm^2$

Exam tip

Although you are dealing with solids, you are finding areas, so all your answers are in square units: cm^2, m^2, etc.

Tax

A percentage of any money that you earn has to be paid as **income tax**. Your **personal allowance** must be subtracted from your earnings first. This leaves your **taxable income**.
For example:
in one week you earn £185 and your personal allowance is £60 per week. You must pay 24% tax on your taxable income. How much tax do you pay?

Take away your personal allowance
£185 – £60 = £125

24% of £125 $= \frac{24}{100} \times 125$
$= £30$

Translations

This just means moving a shape from one place to another. To show how far to move a shape you use a **vector**.

$\begin{pmatrix} x \\ y \end{pmatrix}$ distance moved parallel to the x axis (left or right)
distance moved parallel to the y axis (up or down)

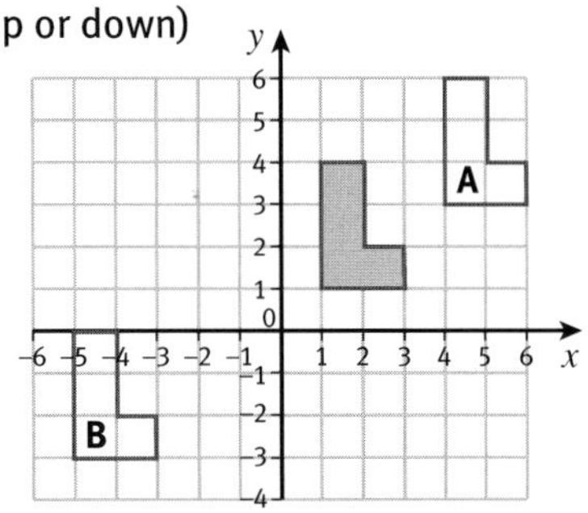

- If the shaded figure is translated $\begin{pmatrix} 3 \\ 2 \end{pmatrix}$ the result will be figure A.
- If the shaded figure is translated $\begin{pmatrix} -6 \\ -4 \end{pmatrix}$ the result will be figure B.

Travel graphs

These graphs plot distance against time to tell the story of a journey. The horizontal axis represents time and the vertical axis is the distance travelled.

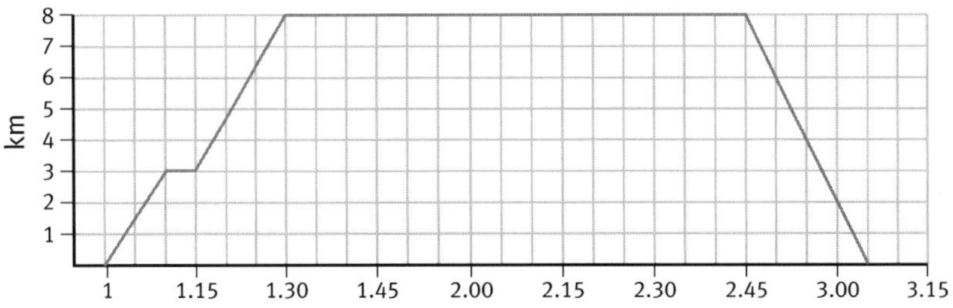

This graph shows Kate's journey to visit her friend Chloe who lives 8 km away.

- She leaves home at 1 pm and cycles 3 km to the newsagent arriving at 1.10 pm. She stops here for 5 minutes.
- She continues her journey and arrives at Chloe's at 1.30 pm.
- She stays with Chloe until 2.45 pm and then cycles straight home arriving at 3.05 pm.

Tree diagrams

Alice catches the bus to college. The probability that it is late in the morning is $\frac{3}{7}$. The probability that it is late in the afternoon is $\frac{2}{7}$.

This can be represented on a tree diagram.

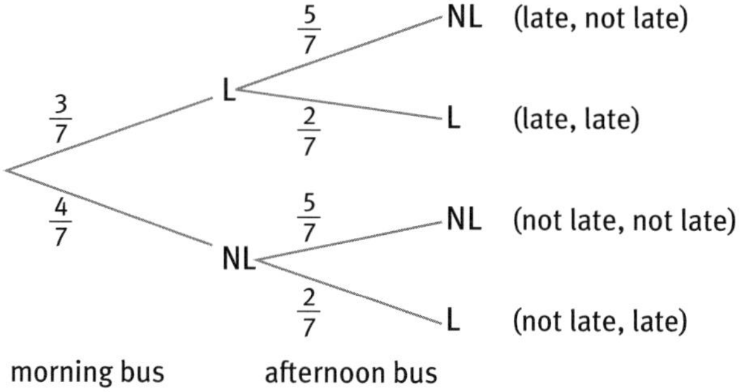

Find the probability that tomorrow, 1 bus is late and 1 bus is not late.

What we need is the probability that the buses are:
(late and not late) or (not late and late)

Multiply along the branches, the **and** rule.

(late $\times$ not late) $= \frac{3}{7} \times \frac{5}{7} = \frac{15}{49}$

(not late $\times$ late) $= \frac{4}{7} \times \frac{2}{7} = \frac{8}{49}$

Add together answers, the **or** rule.

$\frac{15}{49} + \frac{8}{49} = \frac{23}{49}$

Exam tip

Make sure the fractions on each pair of branches add up to 1.
For the example above:

$\frac{3}{4} + \frac{4}{7} = \frac{7}{7} = 1 \qquad \frac{2}{7} + \frac{5}{7} = \frac{7}{7} = 1$

Trial and improvement

This can be used to solve equations whose solutions are not whole numbers.

For example:
find the positive solution to $x^2 + 2x - 4 = 0$, giving your answer to 1 decimal place.

- Try some values:
  when $x = 1$ $\quad x^2 + 2x - 4 = -1$
  $x = 2$ $\quad x^2 + 2x - 4 = 4$
  The solution must lie between 1 and 2
- Substitute values between 1 and 2 into the equation:
  $x = 1.5$ $\quad x^2 + 2x - 4 = 1.25$
  $x = 1.2$ $\quad x^2 + 2x - 4 = -0.16$
  $x = 1.3$ $\quad x^2 + 2x - 4 = 0.29$
  The solution must lie between 1.2 and 1.3
- To find out which of these values is closest, try the value in between:
  $x = 1.25$ $\quad x^2 + 2x - 4 = 0.0625$
  The solution must lie between 1.2 and 1.25, so the correct answer is 1.2 to 1 decimal place.

Exam tip

It is important to give your answer to the degree of accuracy asked for in the question. Too many decimal places or too few will lose you marks!

Trigonometry

This only works with right-angled Δ's

In your triangle, mark the angle you are going to use.

Label the sides, in relation to the angle, opposite, adjacent and hypotenuse.

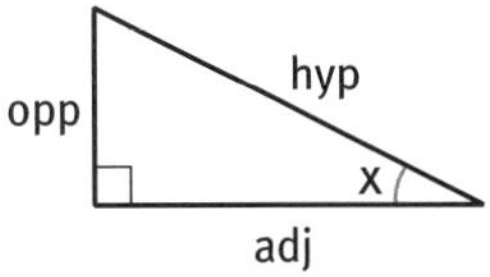

You need two measurements to find a third. Mark on the triangle the information you have been given.

Continued overleaf

Now you must decide whether to use:

sine (sin), **cosine** (cos) or **tangent** (tan). A phrase may help you remember:

S O H C A H T O A (sock a toa!)

or use the triangles

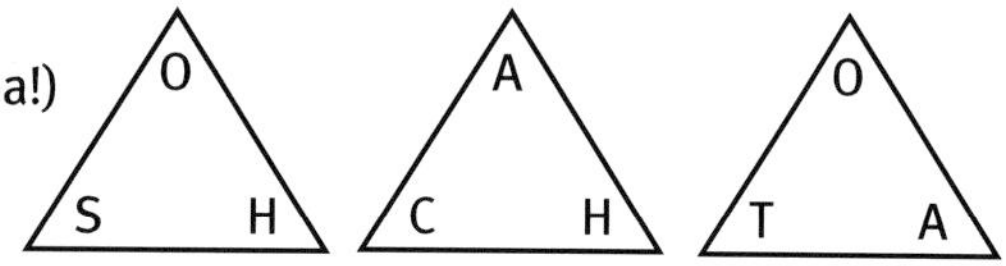

To find the length of a side

Find AB.

- The given angle 64° is **opp** AB.
- The given length is AC, the **hyp**.
- Therefore use sin.

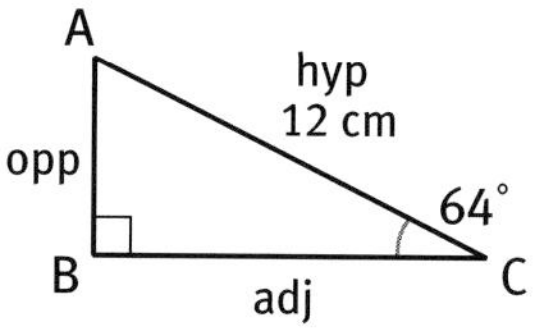

AB = sin 64° × hyp
AB = sin 64° × 12
AB = 10.79 to 2 d.p.

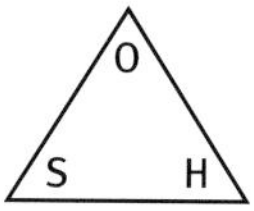

To find the size of an angle

Find CÊD.

- The given length ED is **adj** to CÊD.
- The given length CD is **opp** CÊD.
- Therefore use tan.

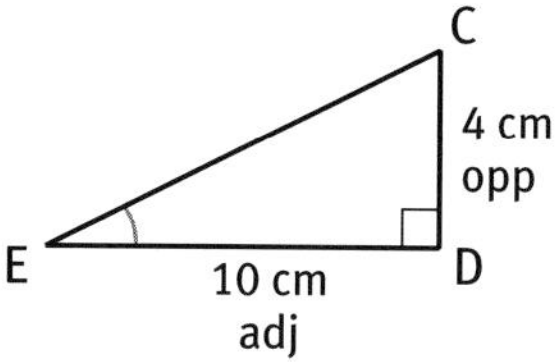

tan CÊD = $\frac{\text{opp}}{\text{adj}}$

tan CÊD = $\frac{4}{10}$

tan CÊD = 0.4 (use $\tan^{-1}$ button on calculator)
CÊD = 21.8°

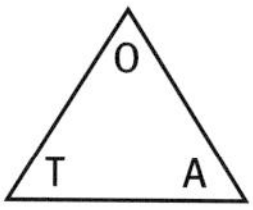

Angle of elevation

From the horizontal looking up

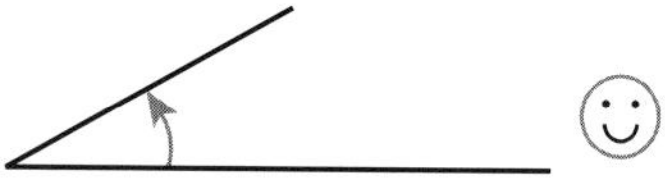

Angle of depression

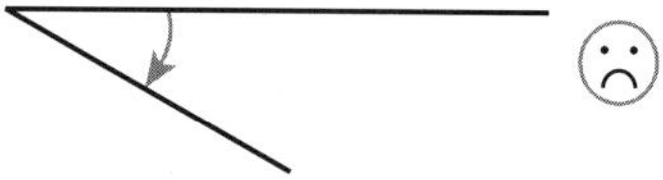

From the horizontal looking down

Units

You should be familiar with the units for length, weight, and capacity. Look them up under the separate entries and learn them if necessary! Always read the questions carefully and be sure to give your answer in the units required.

Vectors

Vectors are best drawn on squared paper. Vectors have **length** and **direction.** Here are some of the basic facts.

a = b vectors in the **same direction** with the **same length**

c = 2a vectors in the **same direction, c twice as long as a**

−a vector in the **opposite direction** to **a** , still the **same length**

$\mathbf{d} = \begin{pmatrix} 3 \\ 2 \end{pmatrix}$ 3 units along and 2 up

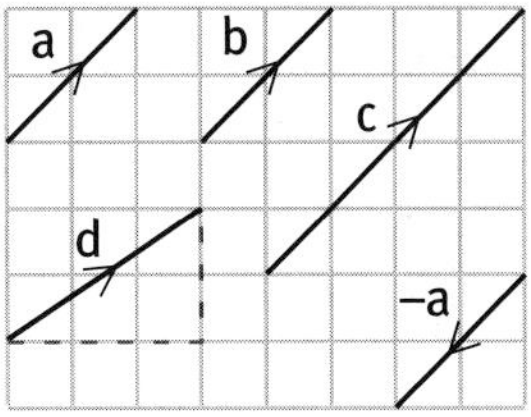

Adding vectors

$$\begin{pmatrix} 2 \\ 3 \end{pmatrix} + \begin{pmatrix} 3 \\ 1 \end{pmatrix} = \begin{pmatrix} 2+3 \\ 3+1 \end{pmatrix} = \begin{pmatrix} 5 \\ 4 \end{pmatrix}$$

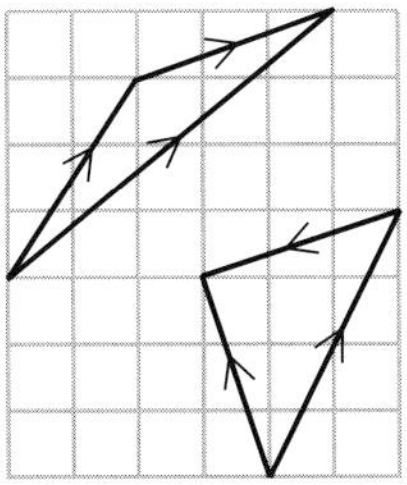

Subtracting vectors

$$\begin{pmatrix} 2 \\ 4 \end{pmatrix} - \begin{pmatrix} 3 \\ 1 \end{pmatrix} = \begin{pmatrix} 2-3 \\ 4-1 \end{pmatrix} = \begin{pmatrix} -1 \\ 3 \end{pmatrix}$$

Multiplying vectors by a scalar quantity

$$2 \times \begin{pmatrix} 2 \\ 3 \end{pmatrix} = \begin{pmatrix} 2 \times 2 \\ 2 \times 3 \end{pmatrix} = \begin{pmatrix} 4 \\ 6 \end{pmatrix}$$

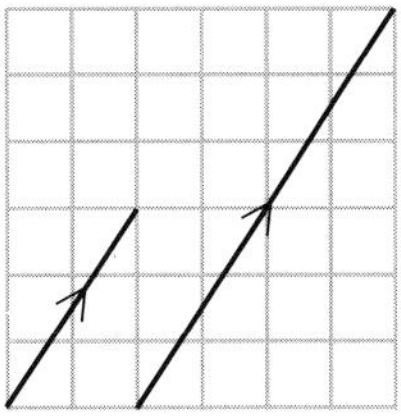

Finding the length of a vector

Use Pythagoras' theorem.

Length of $\begin{pmatrix} \mathbf{a} \\ \mathbf{b} \end{pmatrix} = \sqrt{\mathbf{a}^2 + \mathbf{b}^2}$

Velocity

Velocity is a **vector** quantity, it has both a **size** and a **direction**, while speed has only a size. If you take forwards to be positive, and you ran forwards at a speed of 2 m/s then your velocity would be 2 m/s. If you ran backwards, your speed would still be 2 m/s, but your velocity would be –2 m/s. Running sideways would result in a velocity of 0.

Velocity can be found from a distance–time graph: the gradient of the line is the velocity.

Velocity–time graphs

The gradient of a velocity–time graph shows the **acceleration** at that point. Acceleration is a measure of how quickly the velocity is increasing, and is measured in m/s^2.

$$a = \frac{\textbf{change in velocity}}{\textbf{change in time}}$$

The area under a velocity–time graph is the distance travelled.

Find the acceleration and distance travelled for this graph.

$a = \frac{20}{10} = 2\ m/s^2$

$d = \frac{1}{2} \times 10 \times 20 = 100\ m$

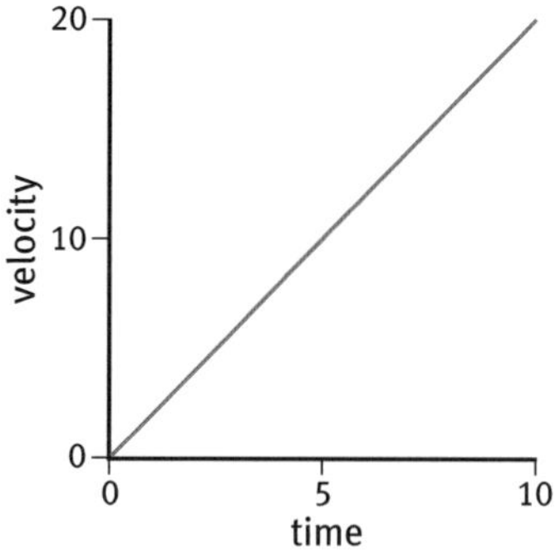

To find the volume of any figure with a uniform cross-section, calculate the area of the end and multiply by the length.

Triangular prism

$V = \frac{bh}{2} \times l$

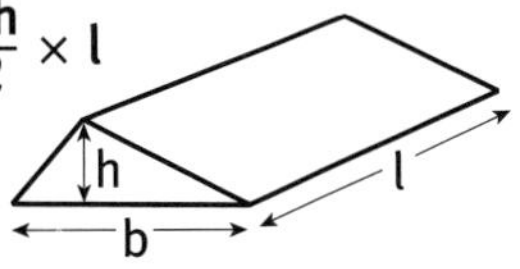

Cylinder

$V = \pi r^2 l$

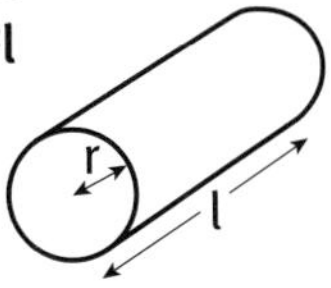

Prism with trapezium cross section

$V = \frac{(a + b)}{2} \times h \times l$

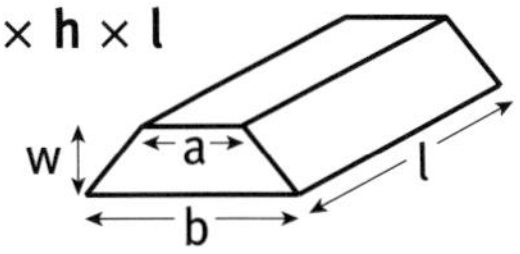

To find the volume of cones and pyramids, calculate the area of the base, multiply by the vertical height and divide the answer by 3.

Cone

$V = \frac{1}{3} \pi r^2 h$

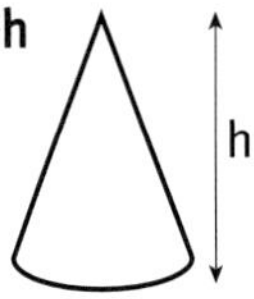

Square-based pyramid

$V = \frac{1}{3} l^2 h$

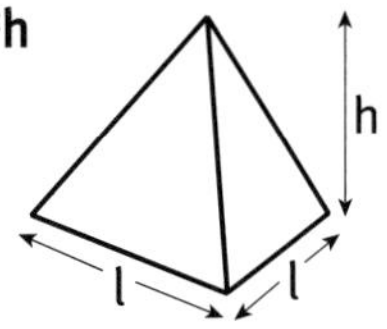

One to learn on its own:

Sphere

$V = \frac{4}{3} \pi r^3$

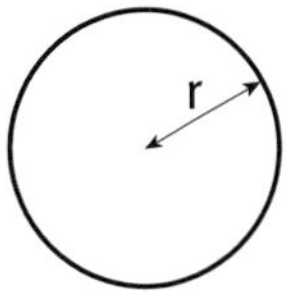

Weight

Metric units

1000 grams (g) = 1 kilogram (kg)
1000 kilograms = 1 tonne

Imperial units

16 ounces (oz) = 1 pound (lb)
14 pounds = 1 stone (st)

You should be able to convert from one set of units to the other.
For example:

1 ounce = 28 grams
so 4 ounces = $4 \times 28 = 112$ grams

Exam tip

You need to learn these.

$x - y - z$

Three-dimensional co-ordinates, (x, y, z)

Remember:

- x units along
- y units back
- z units up.

Always in that order!

A = (4, 3, 2)
B = (2, 2, 0)

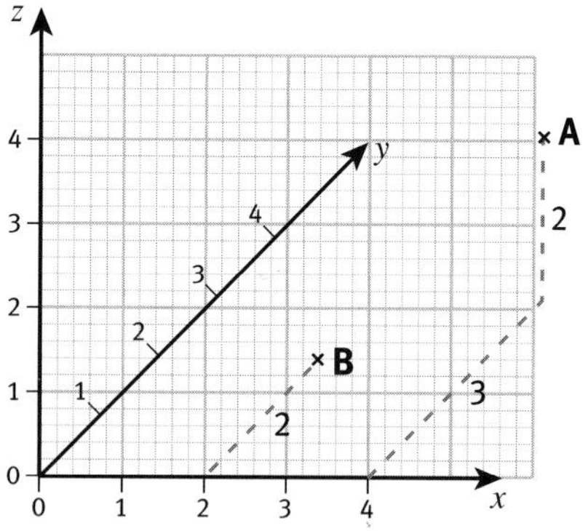